SERVE

Idea-rich strategies for enhanced customer service

BOB 'IDEA MAN' HOOEY
AUTHOR OF, MAKE ME FEEL SPECIAL!

This is the secret to your long-term business success!

Preface

Dedicated to our 'Clients', who may choose, at times, to be our 'Customers'

As you dip into **'SERVE!'** you might notice we have used the word 'client' sprinkled throughout this publication on ***Idea-rich strategies for enhanced customer service;*** in some cases, using both 'client/customer'. This is a *deliberate* choice in our vocabulary and a *foundational* change in mindset we feel necessary to help you enhance your chances of attracting and retaining customers who will become your biggest fans and champions (ie, clients).

Business success (retail, service-based, or even direct buyer connections) is built on establishing mutually profitable relationships; relationships where you make the customer (client) feel special.

When you *'Make ME Feel Special!'* you enhance your chances of converting 'me' from a one-time customer to a long-term raving client and champion.

Client vs. Customer: Aren't they really the same thing?

Webster's defines these *seemingly* interchangeable words

- **Customer:** one that purchases a 'commodity' or service

- **Client:** one that is **'under-the-protection'** of another; a person who engages the professional advice or services of another

Ever wondered why the top performing business owners and sales superstars sell so much better and make so much more money than their counterparts? Plus, they seem to do it much easier, too.

Their secret is in how they 'visualize' and more effectively approach everyone, which results in higher levels of success with their prospective clients.

- **They 'see' clients** vs. customers walk into their locations and act accordingly.
- **They 'see' clients** when they pick up the phone or walk into an office or boardroom.
- **They 'see' clients** when there is a concern or something that needs to be fixed or replaced. They act with a long-term view.
- **They 'see' clients** who gladly become raving fans and champions for them.

Take a moment and reflect on the underlying *'differences'* in the meanings of these two words. The way a person who does business with you can be approached and treated will directly impact your results. In the past, you may have referred to them as customers. **Please think of them as long-term clients!**

Prior to creating our *'Secret Selling Tips'* I thought of them (customers) as clients. This focus was, in part, from the many years of serving my design 'clients' who came to me for help in creating the kitchen, bathroom, or other room of their dreams. This was reinforced from connections with leading selling professionals and top performing business owners and managers across North America who shared this mindset.

Perhaps it would be a *'profitable'* idea for you to follow their lead. The key to this mental shift lies in understanding what **'under the protection'** of another means in your client interactions.

My thought: This means you don't 'simply' sell someone a service or product 'just' to ensure you make the largest short-term profit or commission possible. You **'serve them best'** by helping them fully explore their options to make the *'best possible choice'* when they purchase something or engage a service from you!

You **'serve them best'** by working with them to purchase something that best serves their needs. We need to 'sell' to stay in business and still focus on an important part of the sales/customer service process.

Often, they are not able to clearly articulate what they need. It is important that you, as a top performing professional, work to understand and appreciate what your clients need when they do business with you and your company. The better you do that, the more you will succeed over the long-term. This service or protection mentality also builds solid repeat sales and referral business for you. It enhances your career and makes money too.

When you determine what outcome or benefit is needed (solid qualifying skills), you can gently lead or guide them to that outcome. You become their *solutions* provider as well as their trusted guide. When you do, you become a *'high trust'* professional advisor/advocate who protects them.

This **earned trust** builds a foundation for them to remain your client for life and to become your biggest fan. It also builds a foundation for a long-term valuable client friendship.

In our sales success publications, we've shared that research shows people 'still' do business with those they trust and like. That research remains true in 2019 and beyond. Keep that in mind as you engage with potential and current clients.

One of the secrets to *sustained* business or selling success is to 'maximize' each client relationship by ensuring you demonstrate your 'genuine' commitment to helping them, not just selling them. That mental shift is reinforced when you think of them as 'valued' clients not 'just' customers. The result is they will buy from you again and encourage their friends and contacts to follow their lead in selecting you to serve them.

People love to 'buy' but hate being 'sold'.

Table of contents

The importance of a professional strategic development plan

Whether you are in business for yourself or work for someone else, having a strategic plan covering your professional or business development is essential to your long-term success or employability. Failure to plan is truly, as we've heard, planning to fail! **This is particularly important if you want to attract and retain clients and customers.**

A good plan incorporates several basic components:

- A clear definition of the ultimate objective in mind. **Conceive it complete!**
- A good solid foundation built on understanding of what is required to make it happen by **doing your homework.**
- An **ACTION** plan with specific goals and objectives tied to specific timelines and checkpoints to make revisions along the way.

How do you define your idea or ultimate objective as it relates to your value-added business or career? A little free flow idea generation or creative, blue sky 'dreaming' works. Ask yourself – some **'what if?'** questions to unlock your creativity and help **unlock your full-service potential.**

- What if I could do anything without fear of failure? I'd

  _____

- If I had enough money to ensure my basic living for a year, I'd _____
- If I discovered I had talent, could learn the skills I need to: _____ I'd _____

We cover this in more detail in **'Make ME Feel Special'** available from www.SuccessPublications.ca

6

The answers to these types of questions provide a glimpse into what you'd really like to do; and what may need to change or adapt to get there.

After you've defined your *ultimate desire*, then what? Well, now it's time to start doing your homework and find out exactly what is needed to make it happen or prepare you to act.

Then comes the fun part – setting specific action plans in place to accomplish goals and objectives that will lead you to your ultimate desire – a whole bunch of happy satisfied clients/customers who love you and tell the world about you! **The key here** is to ensure that your goals are clear and specific and can be broken down into even more specific objectives.

An action plan is only as good as its implementation and accountability. This means setting specific timelines for starting and completion of each step.

It also means having numerous built-in checkpoints to allow you to monitor your progress and make any fine-tuning adjustments or course corrections to the plan as you move into its implementation.

Are you serious about 'Establishing a Value-added, Customer Service focused, sustainable business'?

INVEST the necessary time to do some serious thinking about what you want to accomplish, when, and why is essential.

Success doesn't come by accident - it requires strategic planning followed by implementation of your ACTION plan.

'Creating Time to Sell' as a part of your outstanding 'Service' journey

'Creating Time to Sell, Lead, or Manage' was originally created and delivered for the BC Management Team of the **St. John Ambulance** when all their branch managers came together in Vancouver, BC. The objective for our session was a skillful blending of solid business building, sales and service principles with a good use of time to allow their respective teams to be more productive in their customer service efforts. It was very well received. Since then, we've spent time refocusing and expanding it as a tool to offer our clients to help them succeed in attracting, profitably selling, and retaining customers and building referral and repeat business.

The secrets and tools we cover in our on-site workshops have allowed top performing professionals, their managers, and their staff to find ways to be more pro-active in 'reaching' and 'retaining' clients for their organizations. **www.ideaman.net**

While flying to a speaking engagement in the US, I read a study that indicated the **average salesperson put in a 53-hour week and this might be a low estimate.** *Yet, despite this long week,* **less than 8 hours of face-to-face sales activity was recorded (about 15%).** *More recently, I read that the average business owner, leader, or executive had 40-60 hours of unfinished business on their agenda at any one time. Sound familiar?*

Something is radically wrong with this picture. **Work more and produce less** is not a good indicator for any organization that wants to survive or thrive in an extremely hectic and competitive market. Whatever happened to *'work smarter not harder'*?

We are too busy, overwhelmed, and distracted; and that impacts our ability to serve and sell to our clients. We are too busy to invest the necessary time training our staff in their effort to be equipped to succeed.

We are too busy to truly enhance our business and generate and service all the sales potentially available. Sad, really!

To be effective in sales/customer service and business in general, we've been telling our audiences and clients that we must deal with **three areas as they relate to our potential clients.**

- **Pain**
- **Gain**
- **Sustaining**

The degree that you work 'with' your clients/customers to take care of these three areas will determine the impact on your profitability and long-term viability. Each area has its 'specific focus' and profit center. In the sales process, each area has its impact and effectiveness. At times, we work with clients/customers who have one or more of these areas as their focus. The time we invest finding out what their *'real'* need is increases the likelihood that we will be the one engaged to help solve it.

If we only help people with their **'pain'** – will they 'still' need us when it is gone? What motivation do people have to visit a doctor or dentist when they are feeling well? A word to the wise!

Helping them **'gain'** offers a bit more opportunity to serve and build a profitable long-term business relationship built on repeat purchases. What do you help them gain?

If you can work with them through their **'pain'**, help them **'gain'** in the process, and then take them through to helping them grow and **'sustain growth'**, you will become a major, vital part of their team (business or life) for years to come. That is taking full advantage of leveraging your time in the customer service/sales process for maximum return.

They will deal with you time and again, when you help them see and receive the value you provide. I offer it as a mental jog to focus on using your time more wisely and blend some proven sale principles (you've had lots of sales courses) into the mix.

Having said that, how can you focus on the previous success focus tools if you are bogged down with minutia and paperwork or are unwisely using your time each day in non-productive, non-sales-oriented activities?

Ask yourself; no, decide to track and analyze exactly how much time you 'actually' spend in the sales/customer service process. The results will surprise you and they may even scare you!

Many of us in the sales /customer service field find ourselves easily sidetracked. We spend time doing 'paperwork', filling out reports or 'busy work', chatting on the phone, chatting with our colleagues, reading the paper, taking long breaks, and other such 'non-productive' activities.

Am I saying to eliminate these in their entirety? NO! Simply be aware of where you invest your time – and track the results to ensure that investment is well placed. You **'make money'** in business primarily when you are in face-to-face or phone-to-phone sales and/or follow up contact with your clients. **Service!**

You **'earn that money'** by delivering on what you contract and you **'leverage that money'** by good client contact and ongoing service. But first, you need to be and/or keep in contact with them.

- **Prospecting** is good use of time in the sales/customer service process – how much time do you spend doing it? Have you developed a systematic way to track and follow up on each one?
- Have you set aside specific times each day to contact potential clients? When?

- Have you set aside specific times to maintain contact with existing clients to find out when and where you can help them again? **Repeat sales are the best** and the most profitable ones! *I love it when a client I've spoken for calls and asks me to come again. Referrals don't hurt the process either! Many of my clients hear about me from another client, speaker, or trainer and then call to see if I can help their teams.*
- Have you set aside specific time for follow up; to make sure your current clients received what you promised and are satisfied with their relationship with you?

According to **Marketing Metrics** your probability of selling to existing customers is 60-70% whereas your probability of new prospects is only 5-20%. According to the **White House Office of Consumer Affairs** loyal customers are worth up to 10 times as much as their initial purchase. Factor in that acquiring new clients is 6-7 times more expensive than keeping existing ones and you'll start seeing the value of maintaining good customer service.

Customer service is a *success tool* for the top performing professional, business owner, and champion salesperson.

It amazes them when you call – so few salespeople do! It helps convert them into your champions and fans when you follow up and ensure they are happy. When you find out early when something is not working correctly or needs adjustment, fix it!

- Have you worked to make it easier for your clients to find you, get the information they need, and track their order or service process? UPS and FEDEX use on-line tracking systems, which is really a very effective sales and marketing tool. **Michael Hammer** drives home the point about being **ETDBW** (easy to do business with) in *'The Agenda'*. Add it to your sales/service library! How easy are you to do business with?
- We continually evolve our **www.ideaman.net** and **www.BobHooey.training** sites by expanding and

enhancing different customer driven segments. For example, we've added complimentary on-line resources and downloadable articles and videos on a variety of leadership success topics. Visit them today!

- *Our web work is becoming a series of true value-added client-centric sites, as well as very productive and profitable. It is time well spent in creating time to sell, lead, or manage my business and customer contact relationships.*

- Have you 'systemized' your work area and computers to make it easier for you or your colleagues to access information, client files, literature, etc. to better and more quickly serve your clients?

- Have you spent specific time thinking about all the potential challenges or questions that might come up from a prospective client? Have you discussed these challenges and the productive solutions you and your organization provide? Are your staff fully informed and well 'trained' in helping clients with their challenges? Do you have solid, well-researched, value-enhancing answers ready and burned into your mind? Why not?

If you invest even a small amount of time working on these questions and **implementing** the results of your deliberations – you'll find yourself being able to spend more time on the sales, service, and marketing process. Helps you navigate your way through life better too. You'll also find you will attract more clients, receive better quality referrals, and garner more profitable repeat business.

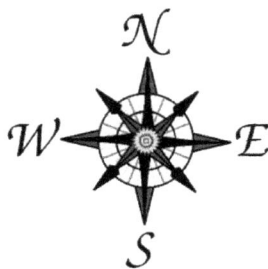

Amazingly enough when you are **'Creating Time to Sell, Lead, or Manage'**, as a part of your customer service focus – you end up selling more and making more money too!

Unhappy customers cost you money – lots of money!

Deciding to focus on making your customers feel special can pay off in so many profitable ways, just as 'not taking care' of them can have negative results for you and the survival of your business.

Let me ask you a couple of questions as we move further into our time together.

What is your average sale or transaction worth? (retail) $_____
What is your average cost to gain each sale? (overhead) $_____

Take a moment and discover how much each (average) client or customer generated for you over the past year. For quick estimates, divide your gross earnings by the estimated client/customer count last year. Take your advertising and other related marketing costs and divide them by customer count.

Let's talk about the value of taking care of each of your customers. But first, let's talk about the real cost of having someone 'unhappy' with your services or products.

A variety of research, (2011 American Express survey) reveals that:

Unhappy customers tell 10-16 other people about poor experiences, (let's use 10 for an average) whereas Happy customers tell on average 5-9 other people about good experiences (let's use 5 on average)

We contend that each unhappy customer 'costs' your company the purchasing power equal to the minimum purchasing power of 16 customers.

Potential cost of making a customer unhappy is at least 16 lost customers... as follows:

Original customer not returning: 1
Customers lost to sharing 'their' horror story: 10
Customers not gained through positive referrals: <u>5</u>

Total customer loss = 16 (minimum)

Now how much is each 'unhappy' customer really worth?
16 x $_____ = $ _____

And how much will it take to 'attract' and 'replace' 16 customers?
16 x $ _____ x 6 = $ _____ Hint: Costs run 6-7 times the annual cost for replacement of a lost client

Add those two numbers to get a real projection of the value of keeping each customer as a happy client.

Now let me ask you another question. How important is it to train your staff to 'effectively' serve each client/customer and to be 'empowered' to keep them engaged, happy, and satisfied?

How much is your business worth? Perhaps you see the reason why so many successful stores have liberal return or service satisfaction policies. What changes are needed to make your policies more client friendly?

What changes would you have to make in your training or policies to ensure you satisfy and retain your customer base? What would it be worth to you to see your customers turned into fans and champions – promoting your business around the world? **What is stopping you?**

Happy, engaged clients/customers are the **lifeblood** of any successful business. They don't happen by accident! They are a direct result of your training and promotional efforts and the experience they receive when they meet you face to face or electronically.

Make a commitment today to better serve them!

Idea-rich Customer Service Tips

Don't just love them and leave them. After you've completed the sale, be available for the follow through. Make sure your in-house co-workers are aware of any special needs your client might have. Make sure you are accessible if your client has any questions. Follow up when appropriate to make sure things are going smoothly. Continue making your clients feel like they are the most important clients your firm has; often, based on referrals, they will be.

When I had my kitchen design studio, I would call clients a month or so after we had finished their new kitchen to schedule an installer visit. The installer would be told to adjust doors, hardware, drawers, and make any small repairs or tweaks on site. If something else was needed, he would let me know and we would order it and he would come back later to fix it. I told my installers, "They will tell you things they won't tell me, because I'm a nice guy. Get them to tell you and then you fix it. That way we both get more work and referrals down the road."

Take the extra time to go over the contract, specifications, finance arrangements, and delivery times to make sure you have covered your clients' needs. This is a good time to catch any mistakes, oversights, or *'I thought you said this was included?'* misunderstandings. Change it now and it's an adjustment. Change it later and it's an excuse or a mistake and stress.

Taking time to explain how something is manufactured will pay dividends. If your client understands the process and lead time, they will be less likely to have unrealistic expectations or demands you have trouble meeting. My boss, **Jack Horner,** would give people a personal tour of the showroom and would take the time to explain how his cabinets were made. I asked him why he did that when he had a good indication they were 'just' looking? Jack told me, *"When I educate them on how better cabinets are made, they know what they are looking at when they shop elsewhere. And often they see the difference and come back to us."*

Customers have needs too

If you are serious about building a successful career and/or sustainable business on the foundations of value-based client or customer service, there are a few areas about customers you may need to know. If you want your clients/customers to receive the best contact with you or want them to be positively impressed with your care and concern for them, read on.

People are unique! Not one of us is the same. We each have different needs. When you meet those needs, *'I feel important or special'* and would want you to keep helping me. There are, however, some needs we all share or hold in common. Taking care to ensure you or your business seriously address these needs will build a solid relationship and a successful career or client focused business.

- *'Make ME Feel Special'* **and valued by you.** How do you do this at present? What changes are needed?
- **Make ME feel comfortable with you and not pressured.** Is this how they really feel? What needs to change to meet this basic need and create this type of atmosphere?
- **Give ME your 'undivided' attention and focus.** This is a tough one, but can you do this? How do you discipline yourself so you can do this? Are there training issues or staffing issues that affect this area?
- **Don't judge ME by your perception of my ability to afford what you sell.** How many times have you caught yourself making this judgment? Each person coming into your place of business is a potential customer – if not now, later. **Treat them 'all' specially!**
- **Focus more on ME than your work schedules activities, rules, or personal life.** This is a business killer! How often have you favored your 'policies' rather than quickly responding or dealing with a customer's needs or problem? What needs to change here?

- **Don't ignore ME for someone who appears to be a 'better' prospect.** Have you ever been on the receiving end of this one? How did it feel? What can you do to ensure none of your customers (especially seniors and kids) feel this way?

Just a few areas where being sensitive to the real needs of your customers will help build a good solid relationship. **Bring them back again and again.**

Ask this question, "Would you buy from yourself?" Why? Take the self- evaluation quiz on the following pages and give yourself an honest appraisal.

Do you recognize good service when you see it?

I read recently that one of the impacts on good customer service is we are not used to recognizing it. Sad, isn't it?

Let's start a customer service revolution! If we want to see our own staff delivering great customer service, perhaps we need to teach them what it is by challenging them to recognize it when they are on the receiving end of it from someone else. If we start recognizing those who give us great service, it will reinforce it for them as well as ourselves.

If you send me the name of the 'customer service superstar' and their email address I will send them a free e-copy of this book with a personal note. Perhaps each of us can find a way to acknowledge them with those they work with every day.

Send them to me: bob@ideaman.net

"Just having satisfied customers isn't good enough anymore. If you really want a booming business, you have to create raving fans." **Ken Blanchard**

What can you do to make this happen?

Conducting an image self-evaluation

"Perception is reality!" This is often the case in our business dealings. People like to deal with people they like or trust. People base their business perceptions on the image we portray. That image is enhanced or blurred by how we act or present ourselves. **How do your clients/customers see you?**

Take a moment and give some honest feedback to yourself, based on your past 3 to 6 months' experience in dealing with your clients/customers. **Hint**: Your answers might lead you to 'unleash' your business potential – and show you where you can improve your client/customer service!

- Is your image one of honesty and straightforward sincerity? How do you know?
- From the buyer's point of view, would you be considered reliable? Why is that true?
- Could you honestly say your customers received special benefits dealing with you not available from one of your competitors? What? Why?
- In their eyes, would you appear to be an expert in your field? Why would they say that?
- Have you been effective in helping solve their problems? How so?
- Would you say you handled complaints to their complete satisfaction? How did you accomplish this?
- Is integrity one of your watchwords? How does it show in your dealings?
- Other than your business dealings, would you think your customers believe you have their best interests and welfare at heart? Why?
- Do your customers look at you as a good reliable source of product or service information? Why?
- Would the majority of your customers continue dealing with your business, even if a competitor offered slightly lower prices? Why would they do that?

- What percentage of your customers or new clients comes from referrals? Why is that number significant?
- How do you plan to keep yourself and your staff educated and current in your field?
- Describe how you keep in touch with past clients. Describe the results.
- Other questions?

If you have been honest in your appraisal of your business operation, you might have seen a few areas in which improvement would help. Go back over your answers and **ask yourself,**

- How can I 'unleash' my business potential by improving based on the answer to this question?
- How can I improve how I seek and service my clients?
- How can I change what I offer them to reflect more accurately what they need?
- How can I make a difference in my career and my community by making the changes I see needed here?
- How can I equip my staff and co-workers to better reflect the changes needed?
- How can I partner with other business owners to strengthen and expand the way we do business and the services or products we deliver?
- Can I reorganize my business to allow myself to enjoy my life better?

Honest reflection, followed by a commitment to act, will perform miracles. Time and time again business owners have done some soul searching and come up with some great ways to re-invent their business and give their clients the service they deserve!

"Your most unhappy customers are your greatest source of learning." **Bill Gates**

Confidence about Credibility

"No one gets taken seriously in this world unless he or she has credibility. Not credibility about brilliant ideas, or heroic deeds, but credibility about daily habits and performance." Anonymous

There are four crucial Credibility Habits

Successful business is built on established credibility. Your customers want to be able to trust and rely on you to do what you say you'll do – when you say you'll do it. Here are the four ways in which we establish our credibility. How would you rate yourself and your co-workers or staff in these areas? Are there areas in which you see improvement needed?

Showing up on time

Time is the most valuable commodity we have. It is precious in that it is finite and cannot be banked or saved – it must be leveraged and used wisely. When you devalue my time – you devalue me! Show me that I can count on you to be there when you say you will and I will begin to trust you.

Doing what you say

Following through and doing what you say is very rare. We expect to be disillusioned, to be lied to, and to be disappointed. When we aren't, we are pleasantly surprised and your credibility soars with us. **Under promise and over deliver!**

Finishing what you start

What a nice surprise, when we discover that you finish what you start. What a difference this makes in the corporate field. Doing this will set you apart from your competition. Resolve to start and complete what you commit to doing if you would build a successful business or career.

Saying please and thank you

Common courtesy is not that common. As individuals, we are too often treated with a lack of civility or respect. Show appreciation for people and their willingness to pursue dealing with you or buying from your firm. This will serve you well and help win their loyalty as a long-term client.

These simple habits may seem self-evident, but the failure to observe them is probably the biggest cause of loss of credibility in business.

In an increasingly competitive global economy, our clients/ customers want to feel special, and they want to be able to trust you. How would you rate yourself and your company in this area? How would you change what you're doing now to ensure they get that opportunity?

Idea-rich Customer Service as a sales tool for higher prices

If you are looking for a way to differentiate yourself from your completion and minimize having to offer discounts, exceptional customer service works. More so if you happen to be a smaller company (or project that smaller, friendly image to your prospective clients). According to a 2011 **American Express** survey 80% of North Americans thought that smaller companies placed a greater emphasis on customer service.

In that same survey respondents indicated (70%) they were willing to spend more with companies they believed provide excellent customer service. They also mentioned (59%) they'd try a new brand or company if it provided a better customer service experience.

What are you doing to create enhanced perceived value in what you offer?

Master, who is my customer?

Many years ago, a young servant came to his wise and rich master and enquired of him how he should be successful in business. The wise Master said, *"By taking care of the real needs and providing value for your customers."* The young servant replied, *"But Master, who is my customer?"*

This *personalized* parable from my Sunday school days illustrates the confusion we all too often have in business. **"Who is our client/customer?"** I would contend that we have both internal and external clients/customers.

External customers are those who would do business with us and allow us to make a profit. Why would it be important to make sure we take care of the needs of our external customers?

Internal customers are those who assist us in making our business successful by playing a part (co-workers, staff) or supplying something we need to be successful. The same question on taking care of our internal customers' needs requires a bit more thought, doesn't it?

Why would it make sense to take care of those who work alongside you in your business or do part of the sales, delivery, or installation process? For your client/customer, they are the company and each time they encounter one of them (touch point or moment of truth), your reputation and referral factor is on the line. Why would it make sense to take care of those who supply you with products or services? None of us work in isolation, do we?

In a pinch when you 'just gotta have it!' – who do you think your suppliers will help? Why? What can you do to build a relationship that returns that response? Are you committed to increasing your effectiveness serving your external customers and internal customers alike?

What makes 'YOU-nique?'

"To my customer, I may not have the answer, but I'll find it. I may not have the time, but I'll make it. I may not be the biggest, but I'll be the most committed to your success!" Anonymous

In a world of increasing 'me-too's' and 'sorta-like's' and 'ditto's' what makes you stand out from the crowd? What **'YOU-niqueness'** do you bring to the marketplace that will make your potential clients/customers want to deal with you and return time and time again? Are there things you do that your clients/customers aren't expecting?

Take a few minutes and give some creative thought to these questions. Analyze your answers, for in them are revealed the secrets of your eventual success and competitive edge.

- What do I provide my clients/customers that **they can't get everywhere else**?
- What can I do to follow-up as a thank you to people – even those who don't buy from me now?
- What can I say or give to my clients/customers that will influence them to remember me and the experience they enjoyed with my firm?
- What 'extra-unexpected value' can I provide my clients/customers after they buy from me?
- What can I give my clients/customers that will totally amaze them – something they would never expect?
- How can I build long term relationships and communicate with clients/customers and their families that will influence them to remember me for years to come?

Based on careful thought – what changes will you commit yourself to making which will ensure these 'You-nique' factors become part of your daily operation? **When will you start?**

Understanding why people buy… how to re-position yourself to take advantage of that reasoning

People make purchases, accept offers, or decide to frequent a specific store or vendor for a variety of reasons. They buy into benefits. The better you understand the reasons they buy, as related to your product or service, the better you will be equipped to convince them to buy from you. Your research and conversations with them can uncover the keys to gaining and retaining them as customers. *'Idea-rich customer service'* is offering me what I really need, not just what you sell or what I ask for!

The following benefits reflect the reasons people buy in order of importance. Remember each prospect is different, as is each product or service. Your product or service might not offer all these benefits. That might be ok, or maybe not – you decide! However, is there some way to modify or position your product or service to offer each benefit?

Unleash your Business Potential – **offer clients/customers more reasons to deal with you! Here are ten top reasons why people make decisions to buy or engage in the services of a professional or business.**

1. To make money/acquire or possess
Describe how your product or service offers me the potential for profit or a potential gain.

2. To save money or prevent future loss
Describe how your product/service offers ways to save me money.

3. To save time
Describe how your product/service can save me time.

4. For recognition
Describe how your product/service offers me recognition or status.

5. For security/peace of mind
Describe how your product/service offers me security or peace of mind.

6. For convenience/comfort
In what ways does your product/service provide for my convenience or comfort?

7. For flexibility
How is your product/service rate in flexibility? In what areas? How?

8. For satisfaction/reliability/pleasure or entertainment
How does your product/service stack up in these areas? Why is that important to me?

9. For status or pride of ownership/ gratify ego or impress others
How does your product/service add to my status or pride of ownership?

10. For health reasons
Is there some way that your product/service will contribute to my health?

Drop me an email and I'll send you the full list of **50 emotional reasons why people buy. bob@ideaman.net**

Understanding the answers to these questions will give you an edge in gaining, serving, and keeping your customers. Being able to present your product or service from the perspective of meeting your client's needs, by appealing to their desired benefits, can be critical to your success.

The more you know about your client/customer, your product/service, and your competition, the better equipped you are to effectively do business. Can you think of any other reasons why people would want to do business with you?

The Seven Be-Attitudes of Great Service

Customer service is one of the *critical* foundations for any enduring business success. It does depend on more than just a catchy slogan to engage the minds and hearts of everyone on your team. It takes leadership and ongoing commitment on the part of owners and managers to show, employees and clients alike, the true essence of enhanced client/customer service.

"Customer Service is not just *'a part'* of your business. Customer service *'IS'* your business!"

A few guiding principles might be helpful. I trust will be of assistance in sharing the importance of customer service all year. I've been sharing them around the globe for the past 19 plus years. Here are my **7 'Be-Attitudes'**.

1. **Be professional** – put the client/customer first. Present yourself and your company in a professional manner. A professional is always looking for ways to help their client and to make their life better by offering products or services that work for them.

2. **Be polite** – wouldn't you expect to be given consideration and respect? Remember to give your clients the same courtesy, regardless of the kind of day you may be having.

3. **Be prompt** – do your best to not keep clients/customers waiting. If you promise something, do everything you can to deliver on time; or call and let the customer know exactly what time to expect you. Try not to keep a customer waiting on the phone or in your store either.

4. **Be proud** – you are an expert, a solutions provider to your clients. Be proud of your expertise and ability to help your clients/customers.

5. **Be personal** – remember your customers are individuals. Don't you hate it when people treat you like just another number? Make a commitment to treat every customer as an individual – it will make them feel special; because they are!

6. **Be persistent** – good service isn't always given on the first encounter. Be persistent in your efforts to serve and solve their problems. If your customer has a problem with your service or product, making sure they are satisfied, or the problem is rectified to their needs is essential.

7. **Be patient** – some clients/customers need a little more time or assistance to make their selection. Taking the time, especially with our seniors or children, is the true sign of a customer service professional.

These *7 'Be-Attitudes' of customer service* will not guarantee you success in business.

They will, however, give you one of the foundations for success in building a business that will still be here well into the next 'decade or three' to serve your clientele actively and profitably.

They will also give you a guideline to lead by example and to train those to whom you entrust your business and your reputation – your staff!

How do you make each of your clients/customers feel appreciated? How do you demonstrate that in each contact?

Turning Client Complaints into $ and sense!

Customer complaints can be a 'gold mine' if handled correctly with the proper attitude and perspective. In fact, they can be an asset to helping you become more productive and profitable. Unfortunately, all too many businesses treat them with less than courteous responses and deal with them as quickly as they can.

Customer complaints and feedback offer:

- **Real (RAW) feedback on your performance.** Using this steady flow of feedback and information can be beneficial to adapting and keeping your business and its policies current and effective.

- **Complain because they care.** It may not seem like it, but clients/customers who complain are demonstrating they care about the relationship and the value you provide. They are also giving you an opportunity to show how much you care and value them. This is your chance to turn them into fans and champions by going the extra mile to take care of their needs.

- **Opportunity to refine your product mix and service.** People's problems, feedback, and complaints can be a mirror to show *cracks in your process* and areas where you can make changes to improve, refine, or adapt your service and product mix. Don't miss out!

- **Opportunity to see new areas of growth or expansion.** Successful businesses are always on the lookout for ways to expand their business by offering more to their clients.

- **Opportunity to be a leader in your field.** Each complaint is an opportunity to see areas for improvement in your business – to better compete and serve their needs. Leaders seize the opportunities and build on them. Are you a leader or an also ran?

- **Opportunity to prove your commitments.** We talk about customer service and taking care of business a lot! But here is a great opportunity to prove firsthand to your clients and staff just how committed you really are to this area of service.

Remember: "If you're not taking care of your customers, your competitors will!" © Bob 'Idea Man' Hooey

Mistakes made by newer (sales) staff

Why is it that senior sales staff are frequently *more effective and more productive* in their sales efforts?

Could it be that they've learned these simple points that help them sell better? You work hard to either identify potential clients to call or to promote your business and its products and services to entice potential clients to visit. When your staff engage them how often do you see your efforts wasted as they walk out the door or say, "No Thanks!"?

The essence of true customer service is a solid commitment to providing them with the most professional sales and service possible. But, there are some obvious pitfalls as well.

1. **Lack of preparation.** There is an old saying: "Success happens when opportunity meets preparedness!"

2. **Not listening**. 90% of salespeople never listen and are doomed to ineffectiveness.

3. **Failing to ask for the order**. Most of the studies I've read show that 70% of all sales folks NEVER ask for the order. Do yours?

4. **Poor or no follow up**. Follow up and follow through is where 90% of all great sales are made.

5. **Small thinking**. Want bigger sales, bigger orders? You must think bigger. Ask these questions: "How high is high? What is my maximum potential?"

6. **Failing to establish and/or maintain rapport.**

7. **Failing** to really commit and establish themselves as experts in their field.

Ask yourself, how you and your colleagues fare on each of these areas? Would you give yourself a passing mark? Which ones would need a little work? How will you change to make sure you give your clients/customers the most professional service possible?

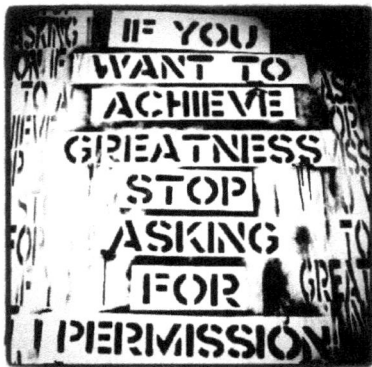

Give your team a chance to win by reminding them of these *success tactics*.

Remind them to keep focused and keep working toward their goals of helping the client make a decision that is good for the client and profitable for the company.

How can you help them make the changes they need to become a professional salesperson and provide value-added service?

Copyright and license notes

Serve!
Idea-rich strategies for enhanced customer service

Bob 'Idea Man' Hooey, Accredited Speaker, 2011 Spirit of
CAPS recipient. Prolific author of 30 plus business, leadership,
and career success publications

Photos of Bob: **Dov Friedman**, www.photographybyDov.com
Bonnie-Jean McAllister, www.elantraphotography.com
Editorial, layout and design: **Irene Gaudet,** Vitrak Creative
Services, vitrakcreative.com

ISBN: 9781998014088 IS

Printed in the United States 10 9 8 7 6 5 4 3 2 1
Success Publications – a division of Creativity Corner Inc.
Box 10, Egremont, AB T0A 0Z0
www.successpublications.ca
Creative office: 1-780-736-0009

Acknowledgements, credits, and disclaimers

תודה
Dankie Gracias
Спасибо Merci شكرا Takk
Köszönjük Terima kasih
Grazie Dziękujemy Děkojame
Ďakujeme Vielen Dank Paldies
Kiitos Täname teid 謝谢
Thank You Tak
感謝您 Obrigado Teşekkür Ederiz
Σας Ευχαριστούμ 감사합니다
Bedankt Děkujeme vám ขอบคุณ
ありがとうございます
Tack

As with each of my books, a very special dedication of this piece of myself, to the two people who meant the most to me, my folks **Ron and Marge Hooey**. Sadly, both my parents left this earthly realm in 1999. I still miss our time together and your encouragement and love. I was blessed with the two of you in my life. I've added **George and Lillian Sidor** (Irene's folks) to this gratitude list.

To my inspiring wife and professional proofreader and publications coach, **Irene Gaudet**, who loves, encourages, and supports me in my quest to continue sharing my **Ideas At Work!** across the world. Thank you seems so inadequate for your timely work in helping make my writing and my client service better! I love the time we spend together!

To my colleagues and friends in Toastmasters, the National Speakers Association (NSA), the Canadian Association of Professional Speakers (CAPS), and the Global Speakers Federation (GSF) who continually challenge me to strive for success and increased excellence.

To my great audiences, leaders, students, coaching clients, and readers across the globe who share their experiences and enjoyment of my work. Your positive and supportive feedback encourages me to keep working on additional programs and success publications like this updated version. My experience with you creates the foundation for additional real-life experiences I can take from the stage to the page, the classroom to the boardroom.

My thanks to a select few friends for your ongoing support and 'constructive' abuse. You know who you are. ☺

Disclaimer

We have not attempted to cite all the authorities and sources consulted in the preparation of this book. To do so would require much more space than is available. The list would include departments of various governments, libraries, industrial institutions, periodicals, and many individuals. Inspiration was drawn from many sources, including other books by the author; in this updated creation of this min-version of **'SERVE!'**

'Serve!" is written and designed to provide information on more effective use of your time, as a business leader's enhancement guide. It is sold with the 'explicit' understanding that the publisher and/or the author are not engaged in rendering legal, accounting, or other Professional services. If legal or other expert assistance is required, the services of a competent Professional in your geographic area should be sought.

It is not the purpose of this mini book to reprint all the information that is otherwise available. Its primary purpose is to complement, amplify, and supplement other books and reference materials already available. You are encouraged to search out and study all the available material, learn as much as possible, and tailor the information to your individual needs. This will help to enhance your success in being a more effective salesperson, leader or professional.

Every effort has been made to make this book as complete and as accurate as possible within the scope of its focus. However, there may be mistakes, both typographical and in content or attribution. Graphics are royalty free or under license. Care has been taken to trace ownership of copyright material contained in this volume. The publisher will gladly receive information that will allow him to rectify any reference or credit line in subsequent editions. This book should be used only as a general guide and not as the ultimate source of information. Furthermore, this book contains information that is current only up to the date of publication.

The purpose of 'SERVE!' is to educate and entertain; *perhaps to inform and to inspire. It is certainly to challenge its readers to learn and apply its secrets and tips, to challenge them to enhance their skills and leverage their efforts to create more Productive outcomes. The author and publisher shall have neither liability nor responsibility to any person or entity with respect to any loss or damage caused, or alleged to have been caused, directly or indirectly, by the information contained in this book.*

Bob's B.E.S.T. publications

Bob is a *prolific* author who has been capturing and sharing his wisdom and experience in print and electronic formats for the past fifteen plus years. In addition to the following publications, several of them best sellers, he has written for consumer, corporate, trade, professional associations, and on-line publications. He has been engaged to write and assist on publications by other best-selling writers and successful companies.

Bob's **B**usiness **E**nhancement **S**uccess **T**ools

Leadership, business, and career success series
Running TOO Fast (8th edition 2022)
Legacy of Leadership (6th edition 2024)
Make ME Feel Special! (6th edition 2022)
Why Didn't I 'THINK' of That? (6th edition 2022)
Speaking for Success! (10th edition 2023)
THINK Beyond the First Sale (3rd edition 2017)
Prepare Yourself to WIN! (3rd edition 2018)

Bob's mini-book success series
The Courage to Lead! (4th edition 2024)
Creative Conflict (3rd edition 2024)
Get to YES! (5th edition 2023)
THINK Before You Ink! (3rd edition 2017)
Running to Win! (2nd edition 2024)
Generate More Sales (5th edition 2023)
Unleash your Business Potential (3rd edition 2023)
Learn to Listen (2nd edition 2017)

Creativity Counts! (3rd edition 2024)
Create Your Future! (3rd edition 2024)

Bob's Pocket Wisdom series *(coming as e-books in 2024)*
Pocket Wisdom for **Selling Professionals**
Pocket Wisdom for **Speakers** (updated 2023)
Pocket Wisdom for **Innovators**
Pocket Wisdom for **Leaders – Power of One!** (updated 2023)
Pocket Wisdom for **Business Builders**

Co-authored books created by Bob
Quantum Success – 3 volume series (2006)
In the Company of Leaders (3rd edition 2014)
Foundational Success (2nd edition 2013)

Bob's Idea-rich leaders edge series (new 2018-2023)
LEAD! *12 idea-rich leadership success strategies*
CREATE! *Idea-rich strategies for enhanced innovation*
TIME! *Idea-rich tips for enhanced performance and productivity*
SERVE! *Idea-rich strategies for enhanced customer service*
SPEAK! *Idea-rich tips and techniques for great presentations*
CREATIVE CONFLICT *Idea-rich leadership for team success*

Visit: www.SuccessPublications.ca for more information on
Bob's publications and other success resources.

Email: bob@ideaman.net or visit:
www.SuccessPublications.ca

**"A man who dares to waste one hour of life
has not discovered the value of life."**
Charles Darwin

What they say about Bob 'Idea Man' Hooey

I frequently travel across North America, and more recently around the globe, sharing my **Ideas At Work!**

I am fortunate to get feedback and comments from my audiences and colleagues. These comments come from people who have been touched, challenged, or simply enjoyed themselves in one of my sessions.

"I still get comments from people about your presentation. Only a few speakers have left an impression that lasts that long. You hit a spot with the tourism people." **Janet Bell**, Yukon Economic Forums

"Thank you, Bob, it is always a pleasure to see a true professional at work. You have made the name 'Speaker' stand out as a truism - someone who encourages people to examine their lives and adjust. The comments indicated you hit people right where it is important - in their hearts. Each of those in your audience took away a new feeling of personal success and encouragement." **Sherry Knight**, Dimension Eleven Human Resources and Communications

"I am pleased to recommend Bob 'Idea Man' Hooey to any organization looking for a charismatic, confident speaker and seminar leader. I have seen Bob in action on several occasions, and he is ALWAYS on! Bob has the ability to grab his audience's attention and keep it. Quite simply, if Bob is involved - your program or seminar is guaranteed to succeed." **Maurice Laving**, Coordinator Training and Development, London Drugs

*"On very short notice Bob cleared his schedule and graciously presented at our meeting when the original Speaker was unable to attend. **Last week Bob set the tone for our two-day leadership meeting and gave us all a motivational lift.** His compassion and true interest in people was clearly evident, making him very credible. He shared some great stories, has a wealth of experience and knowledge and it was a pleasure listening to him. His down-to-Earth style makes it easier to retain the information presented. He also followed up with additional info and handouts, cementing his message of building bridges, not walls. Fantastic job, Bob, and thanks again!"* **Barbara Afra Beler**, MBA, Senior Specialist Commercial Community, Alberta North, **BMO Bank of Montreal**

*"I have been so excited working with Bob Hooey, as he has given inspiration and motivation to our leadership team members. Both at the Brick Warehouse – Alberta and here at Art Van Furniture – Michigan; with his years of experience in working with business executives and his humorous and delightful packaging of his material, he makes **learning with Bob a real joy**. But most importantly, anyone who encounters his material is the better for it."*

Kim Yost, CEO Art Van Furniture, former CEO The Brick

Motivate your teams, your employees, and your leaders to 'productively' grow and 'profitably' succeed!

Protect your conference investment - leverage your training dollars.

Enhance your professional career and sell more products and services.

Equip and motivate your leaders and their teams to grow and succeed, 'even' in tough times!

Leverage your time to enhance your skills, equip your teams, and better serve your clients.

Leverage your leadership and investment of time to leave a significant legacy!

Call today to engage best-selling author, award winning, inspirational leadership keynote speaker, leaders' success coach, and employee development trainer**, Bob 'Idea Man' Hooey** and his innovative, audience based, results-focused, **Ideas At Work!** for your next company, convention, leadership, staff, training, or association event. You'll be glad you did!

Call 1-780-736-0009 to connect with Bob 'Idea Man' Hooey today!

Learn more about Bob at:
www.ideaman.net or
www.BobHooey.training

The Secret of the Seed

My neighbor's farm. There is an *'expectation'* that the seeds they plant will produce the crops they expect. They would be very surprised to plant canola and get barley, for example. **This is the secret of the seed!**

Interestingly, I see people planting seeds for failure and then expecting successful or different results in their sales, business, or life. They are surprised when things fail or don't work to their misguided expectations. **Here is the secret of the seed: you get what you plant, nurture, and harvest.**

Exceptional customer service follows this principle.

- **Plant the seeds** of creative, personal leadership and responsibility;
- **Plant the seeds** of continuous encouragement, to dream and stretch;
- **Plant the seeds** of equipping your team with the tools and the motivation to win;
- **Plant the seeds** of personal discipline and long-term focus;
- **Plant the seeds** of co-operative innovation and competition;
- **Plant the seeds** of high standards and personal excellence in customer service;
- **Plant the seeds** of creating value-added products and superior services we *(customers) actually* need;

...and **harvest** abundance and success at the end of your labors.

What seeds are you planting each time you encounter a potential client?